I Marry You Because...

OTHER BOOKS BY WILSHIRE PUBLICATIONS

Weddings: A Celebration

Planning a Wedding to Remember

Showers

Weddings Memories

All about Him/All about Her
   with Marcella L. Jaegle

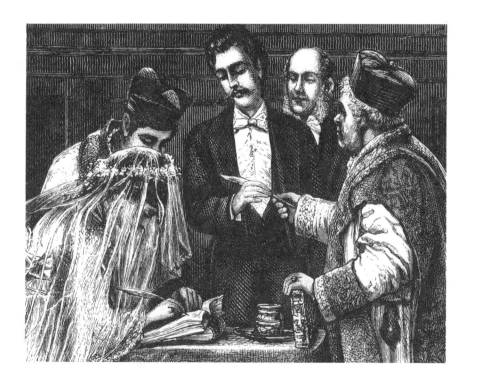

I Marry You Because...

by Peter McWilliams

Wilshire Publications
The Beverly Clark Collection
1120 Mark Avenue
Carpinteria, CA 93013
(805) 566-1425

Published 1990. Second Edition 1993

Original cover design by Paul LeBus
Interior Desgin by Victoria Marine

Printed in the United States by Vaughan Printing
ISBN # 0-934081-15-8

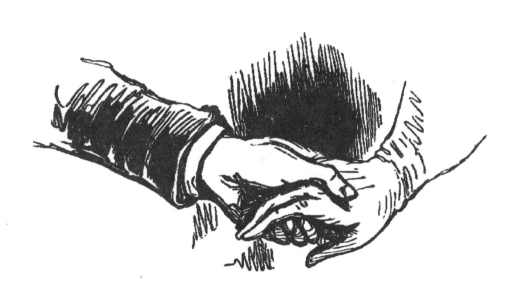

*What do I
get from
loving you?
Loving.
You.*

JOHN-ROGER

I marry you
because
you
are the nicest
thing I could
ever do for
myself.

Think not because you now are wed
That all your courtship's at an end.

ANTONIO HURTADO DE MENDOZA

*I would like to have
engraved inside every
wedding band
"Be kind to one another."
This is the Golden Rule
of marriage and the secret
of making love last
through the years.*

RANDOLPH RAY

I marry you
because
"we"
is better than
"me."

*The great secret
of successful marriage
is to treat all disasters
as incidents
and none of the incidents
as disasters.*

HAROLD NICHOLSON

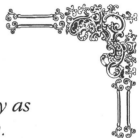

We never live so intensely as
when we love strongly.
We never realize ourselves so
vividly as when we are in
full glow of love for others.

WALTER RAUSCHENBUSCH

I marry you
because
we are such
good friends
you & I.
After being
with you
for only
a little while,
I no longer
relate to
sadness.

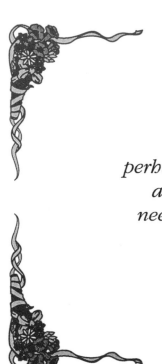

*To be rooted is
perhaps the most important
and least recognized
need of the human soul.*

SIMONE WEIL

Love is a portion of
the soul itself,
and it is of the same nature
as the celestial breathing of
the atmosphere of paradise.

VICTOR HUGO

I marry you
because
together we discover
the secret spaces of the gods.

If I had to live my life over again,
I don't think I'd change it
in any particular of the slightest consequence.
I'd choose the same parents,
the same birthplace, the same wife.

H. L. MENCKEN

*Marriage is a fan club
with only two fans.*

ADRIAN HENRI

I marry you
because
everything
reminds me
of you.

By all means marry;
if you get a good wife,
you'll be happy.
If you get a bad one,
you'll become a philosopher.

SOCRATES

*Love is the greatest
educational institution
on earth.*

CHANNING POLLOCK

I marry you
because
of what I know
and what
I want to
find out.

I think the best thing I can do
is to be a distraction.

JACQUELINE KENNEDY

*Lyndon was the most
outspoken, straightforward,
determined person I'd ever
encountered. I knew I'd met
something remarkable—
but I didn't know quite what.*

LADY BIRD JOHNSON

I marry you
because
I enjoy you.

*Marriage is
the most natural state of man,
and the state in which
you will find solid happiness.*

BENJAMIN FRANKLIN

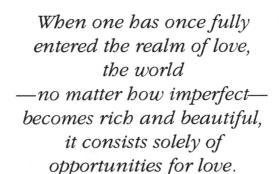

*When one has once fully
entered the realm of love,
the world
—no matter how imperfect—
becomes rich and beautiful,
it consists solely of
opportunities for love.*

SOREN KIERKEGAARD

I marry you
because
in holding you
I am held.

*The bonds of matrimony
are like any other bonds—
they mature slowly.*

PETER DEVRIES

A marriage between
mature people
is not an escape
but a commitment
shared by two people
that becomes part of
their commitment to
themselves and society.

BETTY FRIEDAN

I marry you
because
you are now a part of my life.
In all decisions
you are a consideration.
In all problems
(mostly in terms of solution)
you are a factor.
In all joy you
are sharing;
in all sorrow,
support.

*The intense happiness
of our union is
derived in a high degree
from the perfect freedom
with which we each
follow and declare
our own impressions.*

GEORGE ELIOT

If you have
respect and consideration
for one another,
you'll make it.

MARY DURSO
(MARRIED 58 YEARS)

I marry you
because
we can grow,
not together,
but very
nearby.

The goal of our life
should not be
to find joy in marriage, but to bring
more love and truth into the world.
We marry to assist each other in this task.
The most selfish and hateful life of all is that of
two beings who unite in order to enjoy life.
The highest calling is that of the man who
has dedicated his life to
serving God and doing good,
and who unites with a woman
in order to further that purpose.

LEO TOLSTOY

*Love is the true means
by which the world is
enjoyed.*

THOMAS TRAHERNE

53

I marry you
because
the love
I give you
is second hand:

I feel it first.

Whatever you may look like,
marry a man your own age—
as your beauty fades,
so will his eyesight.

PHYLLIS DILLER

I marry you
because,
considering you,
what else
could I do?

Only choose in marriage
a woman
whom you would choose
as a friend
if she were a man.

JOSEPH JOUBERT

*There is no more lovely,
friendly and charming
relationship, communion or
company than a
good marriage.*

MARTIN LUTHER

I marry you
because,
although
God
created
all things,
God took
special care
in crafting
the rose
and you.

*A successful marriage
is an edifice
that must be
rebuilt every day.*

ANDRÉ MAUROIS

A successful marriage
requires falling in love
many times,
always with
the same person.

MIGNON MCLAUGHLIN

I marry you
because
when you smile,
I forget where I am,
and it takes me
longer each time
to remember again.

It is the man and woman united
that make the complete human being.
Together, they are most likely
to succeed in the world.

BENJAMIN FRANKLIN

In love,
all of life's
contradictions
dissolve and disappear.
Only in love are
unity and duality
not in conflict.

RABINDRANATH TAGORE

I marry you
because
our
union
is a
reunion
with creation.

To keep the fire burning brightly
there's one easy rule:
Keep the two logs together,
near enough to keep each other warm
and far enough apart
—about a finger's breadth—
for breathing room.
Good fire, good marriage,
same rule.

MARNIE REED CROWEL

Love is friendship set on fire.

JEREMY TAYLOR

I marry you
because
everyone sighs at
sunsets and roses.

I sigh at
sunsets and roses
and you.

*Heaven will be
no heaven to me
if I do not
meet my wife there.*

ANDREW JACKSON

I marry you
because
no matter
what the
question,
we are
each other's
answer.

To love is to
admire with the heart;
to admire is to
love with the mind.

THEOPHILE GAUTIER

Love is a taste of paradise.

SHOLOM ALEICHEM

I marry you
because
no one
makes me happier
than you.

*There is no place like a bed for
confidential disclosures between friends.
Man and wife, they say, there
open the very bottom of their souls to each other;
and some old couples often lie and chat
over old times till nearly morning.*

HERMAN MELVILLE

*Love is the heart's
immortal thirst to be
completely known and
all forgiven.*

HENRY VAN DYKE

I marry you
because
no one
makes you happier
than me.

*To decide independently to
live with an equal partner,
and to subordinate oneself
to the formation of
a new subject,
a "we."*

FRITZ KUNKEL

Marriage is the fusion
of two hearts
—the union of two lives—
the coming together
of two tributaries.

PETER MARSHALL

I marry you
because
in you
I am
complete.

*A good marriage is
at least eighty per cent good luck
in finding
the right person
at the right time.
The rest is trust.*

NANETTE NEWMAN

*Marriage is three parts love
and seven parts forgiveness.*

LANGDON MITCHELL

I marry you
because
when we have
joined together,
let no one
put us under.

In marriage do thou be wise:
prefer the person before money,
virtue before beauty,
the mind before the body;
then thou hast a wife,
a friend, a companion,
a second self.

WILLIAM PENN

*Brigham Young is
the most married man
I ever saw in my life.*

CHARLES FARRAR BROWNE

I marry you
because
marrying is
saying
"I do"
and God saying,
"Yes, you do!"

*My most brilliant
achievement was my ability
to persuade my wife
to marry me.*

WINSTON CHURCHILL

I marry you
because
familiarity
breeds
consent.

Of all the home remedies,
a good wife is best.

KIN HUBBARD

Charles is life itself
—pure life force, like sunlight—
and it is for this that I
married him and this is
what holds me to him—
caring always,
caring desperately
what happens to him and
whatever he happens
to be involved in.

ANNE MORROW LINDBERGH

I marry you
because
I need to be
cared for;
but,
more importantly,
I need to
care.

Between a man and his wife
nothing ought to rule but love.
Authority is for children and servants,
yet not without sweetness.

WILLIAM PENN

A coward is incapable
of exhibiting love;
it is the prerogative
of the brave.

MAHATMA GANDHI

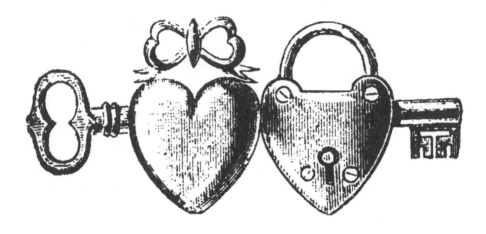

I marry you
because
we believe
in meeting
life's challenges
heart-on.

*Marriage is a partnership in which
each inspires the other,
and brings fruition to both.*

MILLICENT CAREY MCINTOSH

*Love gives us in a moment
what we can hardly attain
by effort after years of toil.*

GOETHE

I marry you
because
I want to
celebrate
us.

In the consciousness
of belonging together,
in the sense of constancy,
resides the sanctity,
the beauty of matrimony,
which helps us
to endure pain more easily,
to enjoy happiness doubly,
and to give rise to
the fullest and finest development
of our nature.

FANNY LEWALD

*A lady of 47 who
has been married 27 years
and has 6 children
knows what love really is
and once described it
for me like this:
"Love is what you've been
through with somebody."*

JAMES THURBER

I marry you
because
when
something wonderful
happens,
I can't wait
to share it
with you.

Marriage is to think together.

ROBERT C. DODDS

*It is a lovely thing to have
a husband and wife
developing together.
That is what marriage really
means: helping one another
to reach the full status
of being persons,
responsible and
autonomous beings who
do not run away from life.*

PAUL TOURNIER

I marry you
because
I believe
I can learn
devotion
faster than
I learned
long division.

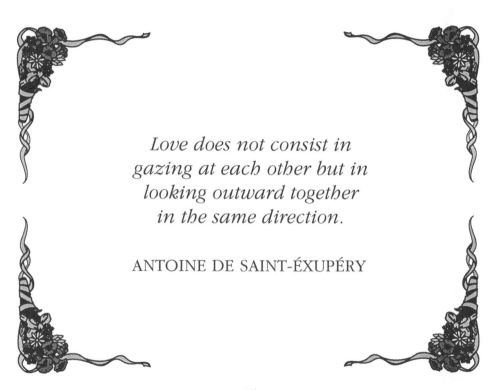

*Love does not consist in
gazing at each other but in
looking outward together
in the same direction.*

ANTOINE DE SAINT-ÉXUPÉRY

I marry you
because
when I hear
the phrase
"dearly beloved,"
I think only
of you.

LUCY: *We have had fun, haven't we honey?*
RICKY: *Yes sir. These fifteen years have been the best years of my life.*
What's the matter?
LUCY: *We've only been married thirteen years.*
RICKY: *Oh. Well... I mean it <u>seems</u> like fifteen.*
LUCY: *What!?*
RICKY: *No... uh... uh... uh... what I mean is, it doesn't... uh... seem possible... that all that fun could have been crammed into thirteen years.*
LUCY: *Well, you certainly wormed out of that one.*

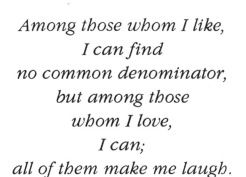

Among those whom I like,
I can find
no common denominator,
but among those
whom I love,
I can;
all of them make me laugh.

W. H. AUDEN

I marry you
because
you make
me laugh.

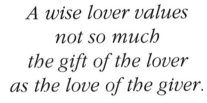

A wise lover values
not so much
the gift of the lover
as the love of the giver.

THOMAS À KEMPIS

To keep your marriage brimming,
With love in the loving cup,
Whenever you're wrong, admit it;
Whenever you're right, shut up.

OGDEN NASH

I marry you
because
I can make
you laugh.

Kindness is the life's blood,
the elixir of marriage.
Kindness makes the difference
between passion and caring.
Kindness is tenderness.
Kindness is love,
but perhaps greater than love,
Kindness is good will.
Kindness says, "I want you to be happy."
Kindness comes very close to
the benevolence of God.

RANDOLPH RAY

I am most
immoderately married:
The Lord God has taken
my heaviness away;
I have merged, like the bird,
with the bright air,
And my thought flies
to the place by the bo-tree.
Being, not doing,
is my first joy.

THEODORE ROETHKE

I marry you
because
marriage is
a state
not to be
entered into
heavily.

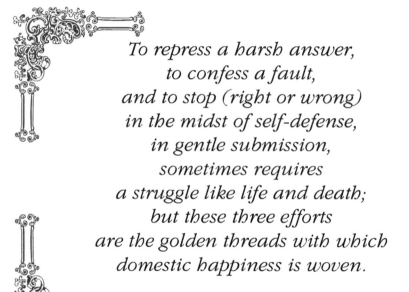

To repress a harsh answer,
to confess a fault,
and to stop (right or wrong)
in the midst of self-defense,
in gentle submission,
sometimes requires
a struggle like life and death;
but these three efforts
are the golden threads with which
domestic happiness is woven.

CAROLINE GILMAN

*The sum which two married
people owe to one another
defies calculation.
It is an infinite debt,
which can only be discharged
through all eternity.*

GOETHE

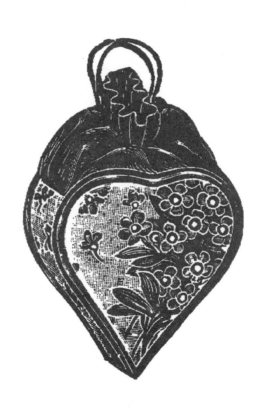

I marry you
because
you give me
the gift of
receiving.

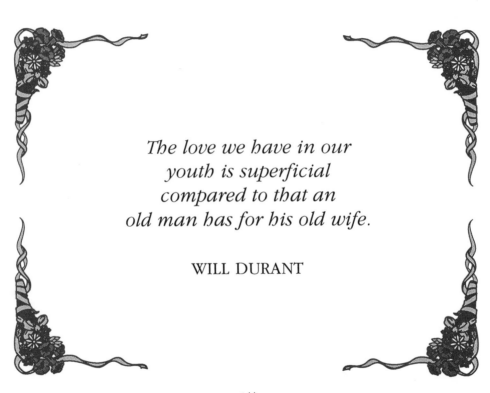

*The love we have in our
youth is superficial
compared to that an
old man has for his old wife.*

WILL DURANT

I marry you
because
in those rare
moments when
all desires
have been fulfilled,
my mind
rests
on only
you.

GUIDELINES FOR DUAL-CAREER COUPLES
WANTING TO AVOID TROUBLE:
Make an appointment to, at least once a week,
be with each other outside the house.
Every six weeks, go away for 36 hours.
To avoid bickering over housework,
sit down and list all household tasks.
Divide them equitably.
Don't set too-high standards for housework.

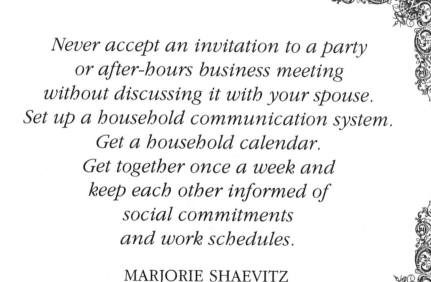

*Never accept an invitation to a party
or after-hours business meeting
without discussing it with your spouse.
Set up a household communication system.
Get a household calendar.
Get together once a week and
keep each other informed of
social commitments
and work schedules.*

MARJORIE SHAEVITZ

I marry you
because
you teach
me things
I never thought
I knew.

An immature person
may achieve great success
in a career
but never in marriage.

BENJAMIN SPOCK

*Love is not a union
merely between
two creatures—
it is a union between
two spirits.*

FREDERICK W. ROBERTSON

I marry you
because
when I hear
the phrase
"sacred union"
I do not
think of the
Teamsters.

*It is a grand experience to be able
to look a hotel detective in the eye.*

H. L. MENCKEN

*To love someone is to see
a miracle invisible to others.*

FRANCOIS MAURIAC

I marry you
because
you are my
miracle.

*There is only
one terminal dignity—
love.
And the story of a love
is not important—
what is important
is that one is capable of love.
It is perhaps the only glimpse
we are permitted of eternity.*

HELEN HAYS

To love is to choose.

JOSEPH ROUX

I marry you
because
commitment
is something
one grows into
and then
grows from.

You will reciprocally promise love,
loyalty and matrimonial honesty.
We only want for you this day
that these words constitute
the principle of your entire life;
and that with the help
of the divine grace
you will observe these solemn vows
that today, before God,
you formulate.

POPE JOHN PAUL II

*Marriage is a mistake
every man should make.*

GEORGE JESSEL

I marry you
because
God loves
our love.

Two such as you with
such a master speed
Cannot be parted
nor be swept away
From one another
once you are agreed
That life is only
life forevermore
Together
wing to wing
and oar to oar.

ROBERT FROST

Hear the mellow wedding bells,
Golden bells!
What a world of happiness
their harmony foretells!

EDGAR ALLAN POE

I marry you
because
we rhyme.

*Marriage is
our last, best chance
to grow up.*

JOSEPH BARTH

*Love is an act of
endless forgiveness,
a tender look
which becomes a habit.*

PETER USTINOV

I marry you
because
you're
The One.

I marry you
because
I love you.

Prelude Press
8159 Santa Monica Boulevard
Los Angeles, California 90046

1-800-LIFE-101

Please request our free catalog.